The Smart & Easy Guide To Real Estate Investing: Investment Strategies & Business Analysis To Make Money Flipping & Renting Properties

Mark Dennison

Legal Stuff

Copyright Information

Copyright © 2013 Checkmate Marketing Group LLC. All rights reserved worldwide.

No part of this publication may be replicated, redistributed, or given away in any form without the prior written consent of the publisher.

Checkmate Marketing Group LLC

Earnings Disclaimer

EVERY EFFORT HAS BEEN MADE TO ACCURATELY REPRESENT THIS PRODUCT AND IT'S POTENTIAL. IN TERMS OF EARNINGS, THERE IS NO GUARANTEE THAT YOU WILL EARN ANY MONEY USING THE TECHNIQUES AND IDEAS IN THIS MATERIAL. INFORMATION PRESENTED ON THIS BOOK IS NOT TO BE INTERPRETED AS A PROMISE OR GUARANTEE OF EARNINGS. EARNING POTENTIAL IS ENTIRELY DEPENDENT ON THE PERSON USING OUR PRODUCT, IDEAS AND TECHNIQUES.

ANY CLAIMS MADE OF ACTUAL EARNINGS OR EXAMPLES OF ACTUAL RESULTS CAN BE VERIFIED UPON REQUEST. YOUR LEVEL OF SUCCESS IN ATTAINING THE RESULTS CLAIMED IN OUR MATERIALS DEPENDS ON THE TIME YOU DEVOTE TO THE PROGRAM, IDEAS AND TECHNIQUES MENTIONED, YOUR FINANCES, KNOWLEDGE AND VARIOUS SKILLS. SINCE THESE FACTORS DIFFER ACCORDING TO INDIVIDUALS, WE CANNOT GUARANTEE YOUR SUCCESS OR INCOME LEVEL.

ANY AND ALL FORWARD LOOKING STATEMENTS HERE OR ON ANY OF OUR SALES MATERIAL ARE INTENDED TO EXPRESS OUR OPINION OF EARNINGS POTENTIAL. MANY FACTORS WILL BE IMPORTANT IN DETERMINING YOUR ACTUAL RESULTS AND NO GUARANTEES ARE MADE THAT YOU WILL ACHIEVE RESULTS SIMILAR TO OURS OR ANYONE ELSES. NO GUARANTEES ARE MADE THAT YOU WILL ACHIEVE ANY RESULTS FROM OUR IDEAS AND TECHNIQUES IN OUR MATERIAL.

Limitation of Liability

THE MATERIALS IN THIS BOOK ARE PROVIDED "AS IS" WITHOUT ANY EXPRESS OR IMPLIED WARRANTY OF ANY KIND INCLUDING WARRANTIES OF MERCHANTABILITY, NONINFRINGEMENT OF INTELLECTUAL PROPERTY, OR FITNESS FOR ANY PARTICULAR PURPOSE. IN NO EVENT SHALL OR ITS AGENTS OR OFFICERS BE LIABLE FOR ANY DAMAGES WHATSOEVER (INCLUDING, WITHOUT LIMITATION, DAMAGES FOR LOSS OF PROFITS, BUSINESS INTERRUPTION, LOSS OF INFORMATION, INJURY OR DEATH) ARISING OUT OF THE USE OF OR INABILITY TO USE THE MATERIALS, EVEN IF HAS BEEN ADVISED OF THE POSSIBILITY OF SUCH LOSS OR DAMAGES.

Table of Contents

Introduction to Real Estate Investment: First Considerations to Make 6
Planning in Real Estate Investment 10
Inquiries to Make Before Investment 13
Choosing and Estimating the Value of Property 16
So Many Laws Regarding Real Estate 19
Your Real Estate Investment Agenda 22
How to Be Inventive In Financing 25
Managing Risks 28
Boosting Your Profit 34
How to Bargain Firmly and Fairly 37
When to Buy and When to Sell 40
What to Do When You Can't Sell 43
Learning How to Flip 46
Foreclosure: a Lamb or a Wolf in Sheep's Clothing? 49
Renting a Property: a Dream or a Nightmare? 53
The Complications of Commercial Investment 56
Taxation for Investors 59
Real Estate or Paper Estate? 62
We Want Your Feedback on This Book! 66

Introduction to Real Estate Investment: First Considerations to Make

You will hear it said many times: investing in the world of real estate is one of the least painful moneymaking routes to follow. This statement holds some amount of truth. By investing a prudent financial sum and dedicating a fair amount of toil towards upkeep or restoration, you can buy and sell a property that earns a significant profit and have the future ahead looking full of hope.

It sounds easy, yet easy doesn't mean without effort.

The greatest obstacle to overcome when you're new to real estate investment is the rate at which you acquire the skills necessary to achieve success. Regardless of where you operate, investing in real estate is a complex procedure, and you can quickly suffer financial loss if you haven't done your research beforehand.

To make the picture a lot clearer, here are the first considerations you should make before starting.

Take some time to think before investing. Consider what financial objectives you intend to reach, and in what time frame you desire to achieve them. Be truthful to yourself about it. It's easy to plan yet harder to do, especially when market prices for homes have been on the rise for a number of years and continue to be. However, as in any sort of market, values in real estate may drop, and when this happens, experience tells us it will take place suddenly and fast.

When you have made up your mind on how much money and time you're willing to invest, make a note of it. Create a plan for your business for the first five years, paying as much attention to detail as possible, and make sure to revise it after the space of half a year and then again at the milestone of two years.

Include in your plan a fair estimate of the money you have available to invest. This will determine which route you should take, depending on whether you intend to employ your main residence or not for your first move. To provide an example, if your initial budget is beneath $10,000, you should plan either to use your primary residence or to buy what is termed a "fixer-upper," a property that requires a certain amount of maintenance.

Of course, if your credit score is good, you could acquire a secondary property without any financial sum paid, apart from a couple of thousand dollars for the closing costs. However, for this to work the market values would have to rise fast and you to would have to sell the property immediately.

This would involve a lot of risk and would put you in danger of facing severe legal and taxation consequences. Another route would be to pay high monthly installments and perhaps spend additional costs on maintenance. But again this would involve high risk and is probably extremely expensive. It's likely that you would lose more money than you had in the beginning, since even though you invested only a little, you are still bound by law until the end of the contract.

This is advised against if someone is just starting off and without experience.

You should also include in your plan an estimate of the risk you're capable of taking. Be truthful to yourself and reflect on your character. While some people prefer to preserve their capital, others tend to go for the highest profit they can achieve in as short a time as possible. Everyone acts differently under the pressure of risk; therefore, you should know well what your personal limits are.

Furthermore, you should know how much time you have at your disposal to dedicate. You should build your relation with the lender, and research the real estate market, contract signing, insurance policies, the fabric of legal rights and requirements, and taxation consequences, as well as all other aspects of investment in real estate.

In case you're still up for the task, congratulations! You're headed towards achieving a significant extra profit, or why not, even earning a full-time occupation in one of the sturdiest spaces in the world of investment. Don't forget that apart from its potential for huge profit, this is also an adventure with its own merits!

Planning in Real Estate Investment

The results of a study tell us that in 2004, 23% of homes sold were bought as investments. This makes sense if put next to the historical market return statistics and the high percent of increase in prices during the last years. Yet there are several routes to gaining profit from investing in property.

What is commonly called 'flipping' refers to purchasing an asset and quickly reselling it for profit. The opposite of this is maintaining a property for a long time to make profit from tax incentives and the potential increase in the asset's value. You should estimate the overall cost compared to the sum saved from being written off taxation. Remember to calculate charges on interest, taxes on property, insurance, maintenance and the rest, as well as the regular payment per month.

Keep in mind the fact that, for several years now, property prices have been on the rise in the majority of markets. However, because interest rates increase too, it's impossible to predict for how long they will keep increasing, or how much. After all, there's no gain without (some) risk!

Setting aside the profits you can make from writing off taxes and by potential increase in value, you can benefit from the rental of your property. However, you should reflect on the time and costs needed to attract tenants and to oversee the condition of the property, as well as for maintenance work.

A different route of investing is with foreclosures, again though not lacking in risk and usually demanding a significant cash capital. Foreclosures take place when the owner of a property is unable to pay off a mortgage, most often in the space of some months. However, it's rare to make a clean profit without risk on foreclosures.

Usually, properties that are foreclosed on require maintenance work; owners who are aware they will soon lose their property seldom care to make repairs and maintain it properly. You should be ready therefore to invest both time and effort in returning the property to a state that would attract purchasers, if you do it yourself, otherwise money and effort towards employing a contractor that you trust.

The same goes for investing in property that has been abandoned, in this case including the legal know-how before you act. Often, foreclosed properties are under clear title; the bank, mortgage company or similar financier that is the lender claims the title during foreclosure. Sometimes it's not obvious who owns a clear title for properties that have been abandoned. You should foresee that time will be required for research and probably for legal procedures beforehand.

If you wish to make profit in real estate without having to spend cash or sign a huge amount of paperwork and worry over the state of the actual property, there exist investments that are solely on paper. With the advent of computerized information and the vast increase in investing options since the Eighties, a number of new modes of translating real estate into money have appeared, like real estate investment Trusts. These include asset-backed mortgage securities, property bonds investments, mutual funds, trusts and stocks especially drawn for real estate. The place to turn to before taking a step towards investing in such non-property agreements is an individual broker or firm.

Inquiries to Make Before Investment

The world of real estate investment is quite complicated. Every aspect of it falls under a number of legal conditions, in the majority of countries, and every arrangement involves numerous persons, and often involves legally protected and conflicting interests. But the potential to make great profit exists, and in a sense more so here than in other businesses.

Before setting out, try answering the following:

1. What is the amount of money I have at my disposal?

As its name suggests, investing in real estate is indeed, first of all, an investment. Whether small or big, it nevertheless requires a starting capital. You may plan, but having put your signature on paper, you're bound by law to any potential scenario that may arise. For this reason you should have a significant amount of money to invest, from past savings or financing through borrowing and paying interest. How much that is will be defined by your specific situation. What is the amount of money you already have in savings? What is the amount you can lose without being financially destroyed? What is the amount you could put yourself in debt for and what is the amount of interest you can afford to pay?

2. How well do I cope with the pressure of risk?

The concepts of investing and being at risk are inseparable. An investor whose savings is $5,000,000, for example, may suffer the risk of $500,000 without seriously endangering his position. An investor hoping to multiply the $5,000 they have gathered with difficulty into $50,000 constitutes an entirely different case. This doesn't mean the latter should give up and turn away. Coping with the pressure of risk is a great quality in a person, but one has to be fully aware how much money they're able to invest. Remember that the emotional risk is tantamount to the financial pressure. You might be a high-risk flier, or you may be a safe-move player.

3. What are my financial objectives for the future?

A number of investors favour the preservation of their capital, while others prefer to make great profit in as short a time as possible. Both approaches have their risks and demand a specific amount of time from the investor. You shouldn't invest in real estate if you expect a 10% profit within the space of a few weeks. If you desire to achieve a high score of profit, bear in mind that it is possible but often demands the dedication of a year's work or more. For that duration, your money isn't liquid unless you decide to borrow against it. Apart from your capital being restricted for other needs, the value of a property might rise or drop drastically in no time. In most countries, the prices have been going up during the last several years but the change in interest rates can and probably will affect them.

4. Have I reflected enough on my personality?

Investing in real estate requires the ability to tolerate risk, to dedicate effort and time, and to pay particular attention to detail, especially details of a legal nature. But the most important skill needed is the willingness to learn the rules; market research, advertising, paperwork signing, the laws on property and even basic knowledge of human psychology. No one suggests you need to be an expert on all these before starting out, but if you're not in the frame of mind to learn about these aspects and master other elements of the business, you're about to find out about financial loss the hard way.

Congratulations if you're still brave enough to continue reading! You're preparing to make a profit in one of the most ancient businesses still prevalent on the modern face of the planet.

Choosing and Estimating the Value of Property

In modern times, the practice of real estate investment is much easier and significantly more profitable than before. However, even within a sturdy market that offers innovative approaches to estimate the potential profit of property, the possibility of great financial loss in a short space still exists. If you wish to multiply your chances of winning, take a look at the following advice:

The Internet has drastically remodeled the possibilities of encountering "rough diamonds." There's endless information online with descriptions, photographs and prices regarding properties a street away from your home or on the other side of the globe. Be prepared to pay the fees of a realtor though, if you're not looking only at "For Sale by Owner" advertisements on eBay, Windows Classifieds or Google Base.

A good move would be to pay Realtor a visit, or any estate agent's business. If it's within your budget, acquire a Multiple Listing Service to obtain the same info they do. (This might require a license in some countries, even if you possess the financial capital.)

Be ready to physically visit a property and its neighborhood even if you're employing the Internet to find it, since it's the best way to form a sound opinion. Does the area look respectable enough for the selling value not to drop? And while you're there, keep an eye out for rental signs or even strike up a conversation with the people in the neighborhood.

A permanent resident there might inform you about problems that might not be visible at first glance. Visit the property more than once, under different weather conditions and at different times of the day. These factors play a significant role in how a property looks under different circumstances.

When it's raining, don't despair – it's the best time to visit the property and see whether it has a leaking roof. Making that additional effort will perhaps save you from making a bad decision. The more you know, the better you stand.

Once you have informally inspected the property, it's time to employ a professional to give you satisfactory feedback. Don't mind paying a little extra to someone with experience who will conduct a formal inspection, as it will be an advantage to you, especially if you employ them many times in the long run. If you can, learn everything about how to make a professional inspection yourself, or at least enough so that you won't be tricked by an inspector, although that's very unlikely.

Pay great attention to the details of the inspection report. Not everything in the property has to be perfect, but you should be aware of every problem, big or small: faulty plumbing systems, stained carpets, damage to the wall or flooring, broken air conditioning or inoperative heating systems. Pay attention especially to stagnant water in the basement or close to the foundations.

Remember, all this can be negotiated. No one in particular is obliged to pay the costs for maintenance. But also expect to end up paying for repairs; only rarely is a property flawless, even if it's new. Most likely if a property is perfect it will be too expensive for you to make a profit from it, unless you plan on holding onto it a long time.

So Many Laws Regarding Real Estate

You guessed it right: legal restrictions are more abundant in real estate than in any other business. Due to the large sums involved, and the significance of property serving as living or working quarters, the regulations around it are complex and there are numerous parties interested in securing their profit.

If you want to take a look at the history of property you have to go back to 3,000 B.C. and the Sumerians, long before its recent evolution. All around the world, there's a plethora of laws revolving around every single facet of property. Funding, purchase and sale, rights of tenancy, environmental issues, taxes, even the very definition of what counts and what doesn't count as property fall under a vast number of laws, many of which are not what one would call "clear."

You, however, as the investor, will need to obtain a confident knowledge of laws regarding property if you're interested in making a profit in the long run. The best possible starting point is the contract.

Every contract in real estate requires mutual assent; that is, all parties have to sign a written agreement of exchange. The contract needs to name who the involved parties are, what property is exchanged and for what amount of compensation. The contract must be signed by individuals who are of sound mind and legal age. The contract also has to be enforceable, by consideration. This means the property's value should be as the seller and the lender state, determined by professional evaluation (at least in approximation).

To provide an example, buying property and quickly reselling it is, of course, legal; but not buying a cheap property that is full of flaws and collaborating with a mortgage broker to forge documents exaggerating its value… A governmental body that would guarantee a loan on such a property would look further into the matter. And fraud is punishable by law.

Bear in mind that commercial properties fall under completely different rules regarding their sale and the manner in which they are used. The tenant, also, in the majority of countries around the world, has specific rights regardless of the specifics of the contract.

The lender must comply with a set of complicated regulations, which govern the amount of capital that is permitted for lending, the necessary contracts regarding title, insurance and even the limits to the advertisement that can be made, as well as the offering of funding.

Laws on taxation make things even more complicated. Unlike the tax lien against a car or a boat, it is highly common in real estate to have to clear a lien before title of a property can be successfully transferred.

Therefore, if you're considering investing in real estate, make sure to have done your research on estate law, long before it comes in handy. This way, it will be less expensive now than later.

Your Real Estate Investment Agenda

After the 1980s and the rampant expansion in production, the diversity of investments that can now be made has escalated. It is a professional's task to filter through the technicalities and weigh the risks against possible profit. Nevertheless, an investor with experience doesn't need to have a degree on the subject, but can still turn the odds in his favour if he pays attention to the following sound advice.

Some suggest that of first and foremost importance is the diversity in your investment agenda. Bonds, stocks and other means of savings constitute only one aspect of a much larger rostrum. The general rule states that of your available financial capital no percentage of more than 30% should be invested in a sole division.

Direct commodity investments are regarded as a safe choice only for knowledgeable investors who are capable of holding an overall view of the market. Regardless of its particular target – oil, gold or other – this market constitutes the area with the most risks and dangers. A number of routes exist in real estate if you wish to take a "paper-inclusive" approach in your plan. Mutual funds that are commodity-oriented, Real Estate Investment Trusts (REIT), options or other mortgage-backed investments offer less risk, yet they are advised against for the inexperienced investor.

A REIT is a security body that invests in real estate, such as in company buildings, shopping centers or hotels. There typically are three types of REITs. Equity REITs either possess or invest in real estate and produce profit for investors from the rent their properties generate. Mortgage REITs act as lenders towards owners of property or developers; alternatively they invest in financial mechanisms, which are backed by mortgages on real estate. The third category, Hybrid REITs, form a mixture of both. In order to attest the qualification, a company needs to pay ninety percent of its income to its shareholders per year and invest a minimum of seventy-five percent of its real estate assets, producing at least seventy-five percent of its income from investments in real property or from mortgages on such.

Another route is options. An option is the sum offered by a potential purchaser to remove for some time a property from the market. Generally, options range from between several hundred dollars to several thousand, although bigger and smaller sums also exist. Options legally bind either one of the parties involved or both, in which case they are bilateral and each party is required to fulfill certain conditions. These concern potential issues regarding inspections or the financing, and fall under a deadline.

23

Of course, all contracts differ and if the option hasn't been exercised by the deadline, the prospective purchaser loses the financial capital. This involves a lot of risk but also promises high profits, since you eliminate opposition from other buyers. The positive side of an option is that it allows you enough time to find a purchaser for the property and then sell the option. Therefore you don't have to pay the cost of transactions or try to maintain a debt limit. Research always pays.

Now for the other aspect of your agenda – the "real" one. Throughout history, the purchase and sale of property has been one of the ventures proven to make the greatest of profits with the least risk. Note, "the least risk," not "any risk at all." There's always risk in investment. Prices might rise or drop, following other products or investment factors.

Maintain an open attitude towards learning about the market and the legal procedures involved. Buy and at the same time reduce as much as possible the costs of agents' fees, interest rates, maintenance, etc. Have a significant sum in cash ready as well as liquid assets, so that you can wait until the right moment to sell. If you follow this advice, you won't regret including real estate investments in your agenda.

How to Be Inventive In Financing

In the past, the drill in financing the buying of a property was eighty to twenty. 80% on loan, 20% paid. The rates varied, but 20% was regarded as the minimum limit. The good news for you is that this happened in the past.

Nowadays there exist numerous routes to go about financing the purchase of a property, regardless of whether it's an investment or intended to be used as your home. An often-used practice is to have more than the one loan, often as a second mortgage. The purchaser puts in the sum of 5% and borrows the remaining 15% separately, from a second loan, often at a greater interest rate than the first.

The positive side is that you invest less on the same property; the negative isn't only the greater interest rate but the private mortgage insurance, which the lenders usually require, since the purchaser hasn't met the minimum 20%, and, as you imagine, the fees are quite high.

In theory, the lender may lift the private mortgage insurance requirement if enough payments have taken place, but this is often not the case. When the loans have been paid and the ratio between loan and value is at 80%, lenders might consider taking out the private mortgage insurance requirement from the payments that take place per month, but usually the loan is financed again or the property is sold before this happens.

If you demonstrate ambition, you'll discover other sources to support your financing. For example, when a property is within a newly developed area, the manufacturer might wish to finance a residency loan for an early purchaser. Usually these come in at about 5% of the buying price.

If you're a bold investor, you may obtain a property and sell it without actually being its owner, or at least not for a very long time. You may buy the property, settle a contract, and sell the contract for a range of between five hundred dollars to five thousand, without being the owner of the title. This way you would make a smaller profit but faster. For such contracts, however, you need to have a perfect credit score.

Another route you might pursue in financing are "Sub2" deals, which normally mean that a property will be deeded to you by the seller while the mortgage that exists remains as is. You're not responsible for the loan legally, but continue making the payments. There exist many different types of this new manner of purchasing property, but they aren't suitable for fresh investors.

Another way of financing is by establishing a limited partnership, with specified arrangements defining the rules. Sometimes both partners put up the percentage of costs, often half-and-half, and other times profits are divided according to the unequal percentage each partner invested. It's also possible that one of the partners is the sole investor, while the other partner provides services such as maintenance on a "fixer-upper," depending on the different agreements.

There also exist certain government loaning schemes for individuals with low income, who are in military service or fulfilling other special conditions, though normally they apply for those while intending to live in the property.

You could even finance the buying of a property using credit cards, although the negatives of this are quite apparent. Setting aside the greater interest rates, keep in mind that the lender, before giving a loan, checks all outstanding debts. Withdrawing a cash advance for the 5-20% that has to be paid will probably not grant you the loan.

Family and friends, or any other source of money are regarded by the bank in the same manner, unless of course you can convince them that the financing comes from gifts and not a relative's loan to you. But mortgage lenders expect everything, so you shouldn't try to trick them in any way!

Managing Risks

In the business of real estate there exist different milestones between starting out and being ready to sell. When you're at the stage of looking at properties you should estimate the sum you're able to use, the current state of the market and your knowledge regarding the different parts of estate investment.

First and foremost you should be familiar with the laws. Either new or old in the world of investing, there is no greater threat for you than lacking knowledge of the rights and rules involved. You don't have to become an expert, just suitably competent.

Once you have researched the market, the next step is to predict the possible future. Property prices have been on the rise for years now. However, this can't go on indefinitely. Nobody can tell you for how long it may go on, yet you can look for specific signs.

Is the current economy in a state of stillness or heading upwards? Does the average individual have good employment chances? At what rate are new residences constructed, in comparison with the previous half-decade? These factors should give you a picture of whether prices will keep rising, remain steady or perhaps drop.

After buying a property, there are several things to do to reduce the risk of owing more than its worth. When you buy, make sure to invest with a big payment. Aim to put in a minimum of ten percent. You will have instant equity and obtain a lower interest rate.

During the stage of considering financing options, reflect on how long you plan to maintain the property. Adjustable rate mortgages will help you to spend less cash and enjoy a low rate. They come for one, five or seven years, and in each case the number depicts for how long the rate will be good, while afterwards lenders alter it in accordance with current interest rates.

However, if you plan to maintain the property after the initial stage, you may see your rate rising. In that case, if you don't sell or haven't made sure to pay the principle in the frame of time offered, you might come face to face with greater payments per month.

While ARM rates are rising quickly, property prices are bound to remain the same or drop, due to the interest rates climbing higher. In this case your investment suffers doubly. The rates might always drop, of course, yet that's rare and correction happens often during a fixed rate.

Therefore you should invest up front as much as possible, make a minimum of one additional payment every year and strive for mortgages with a fixed rate and of a minimum length that you're able to afford. A mortgage of fifteen years can pay down the principle faster, allowing you to spend less money on interest, grow your equity score rapidly and often at a smaller rate.

So, look into the future. The world of real estate still counts as one of the most profitable and involves the smallest risk ventures.

The life of an investor is a hard one. Increasing insurance rates, legal liabilities, worrying about security and rising interest rates might not deliberately aim to give him a heart attack though it definitely seems so. Managing the risks has greatly to do with reducing your worry by facing the aforementioned and other factors creating stress.

The first step is to research local markets and the overall economy in as much detail as possible. Do the same for a property. Get informed about the rates of construction of new residences and on the percentage of new sales among existing ones. Make sure to discuss with other, local owners of property your plans and worries.

During construction, lift the pressure by inspecting the demand within your trade area. Focus on the specifics of sites, review competition you might face locally, and compare the differences with other regions. Ensure you're informed about future environment-related schemes.

You should have enough money for insurance, and better to have too much than not enough.

Enter an arrangement with as much money as possible, making sure your resources are concentrated in not too many ways. Make sure you borrow only a little and steer clear of adjustable rate mortgages, unless they apply for more than three years and you're planning to sell before then. Adjustable rate mortgages contain a greater risk, especially those that only involve interest, because rates usually rocket up faster than they drop in the long run.

If you've opted for an adjustable rate mortgage where payments per month are required and are constantly on the rise, because of the increase in interest rates, and at the same time the market price is falling, it's probably time you decided to sell. The preservation of your capital is the most significant factor in investing, even if it requires you to keep liquid during a rapid market decline.

A number of lenders will permit you to borrow more than the one-hundred-percent value that the property is estimated at. But you should put yourself in that debt only if you're capable of employing the additional money to compensate for the price of interest and further charges.

Put effort into choosing parties that are worthy and reliable; don't hurry to settle for a title company with a presumptuous attitude or that doesn't cooperate. Look forward to maintaining good relations over a long time, or else prepare for financial loss in the long term.

The pressure of risk can be distributed between partners, or even between members of a bigger alliance. The benefit of incorporation is that you will be able to keep your personal assets separate from business assets, being protected in the scenario of a general collapse. However, there are restrictions too – your inclusion in incorporation doesn't permit you to elude common debts. A partner though can enhance your position in the long run, if you choose to collaborate with someone you trust and can be productive together.

Your own knowledge and experience would benefit greatly from the inclusion of a partner, aside from the extra capital they bring in and the opportunity to discuss strategies with them. But you shouldn't make a hasty decision. If your approaches differ, you might find yourself stuck or unable to act when it's definitely the right time to. Don't forget, risk and gain always go hand-in-hand.

Boosting Your Profit

Everyone, in any kind of market, aims to buy at a low price and sell at a high price. Only some succeed, since theory is not the same as practice. So if you want to be on the winners' side, reflect on the following ways to boost your profit.

The rule for obtaining as high a profit as possible is this: make sure your costs can't be any lower and find those clients paying more than the rest. To reduce the costs first of all, do as much of the work as you can by yourself, starting with inspection and maintenance.

Learn how to conduct a professional inspection, and even obtain the relevant license. An inspector is paid up to a few hundred dollars for his professional report. By conducting an inspection yourself, you can save thousands of dollars by rejecting money-losing deals without paying an intermediary, and by knowing about flaws that would help you negotiate in a bargain.

Having bought a property, conduct the necessary maintenance yourself if you're able to do the work properly. Poor repairs will only lose you more money in the long run. Compare stores' prices for materials and deals offered. If you're not capable of doing the work yourself, employ skillful workers from small businesses. Companies whose deals include overhead expenses just make your costs grow higher.

Look around the market for small-scale loans by lenders who are not so widely known, to avoid the higher fees of banks and mortgage companies. You should never pay any sort of application fees. The same goes for insurance and title. And no one obliges you to employ whoever the lender recommends to you.

Furthermore, don't settle for paying exaggerated fees when there's no need to. It is ridiculous to be asked to pay $50 to have some papers delivered to the other side of town, and yet it happens all the time. Put effort into choosing a property, the lender, a title company, insurance brokers or an agent. Be as careful as you can.

Do your research on real estate laws and learn the basics of accounting. The equivalent professional will charge you enormous fees for their services, and with good reason. Their advice can save you a lot of money by preventing expensive mistakes. Much of what they do though, you can do by yourself if you learn how. Brace yourself with patience and the desire to learn, and you're on the right way.

When a property has caught your eye, make sure to negotiate boldly yet with clean hands. Be honest about your intentions and be ready to settle for a compromise. If the other party feels they've been tricked, they may sabotage your profit with actions you will only later find out about.

When you're selling, do the same shopping around and bargain for agents' percentages, closing costs and other expenses.

Make sure your property is in prime condition to be sold for the highest price; ensure it's clean, decorate it with flowers, keep the lights on at all times, play music at a low volume, maybe give away posters with photographs of the property to visitors, or even offer them a snack!

Advertise your property widely to attract a great number of potential purchasers. Competition between them will work in your favour. Be prepared to wait during this period, for it is known that if you rush, you will only earn a smaller deal.

How to Bargain Firmly and Fairly

Without a doubt, a negotiation that you later won't regret is the most difficult part of the procedure. It's uncommon for an investor to claim that afterwards they are always satisfied with what they received and that they obtained the price they wanted. But bargaining is something that can be learned, just like any other skill.

Keep information and knowledge in mind; research the market, the law, and all the information regarding your seller's situation.

Include in the latter the knowledge of whether he's in foreclosure or about to be so. Are there any occurrences in his life that dictate a quick sale that is a bargain for you? Just how keen is he to settle? You should also know for how long the offered property has been on the market, what your competition is and what offers they make. Also, if possible, be aware even of the amount of their debts, or how much cash they have available at the specific time.

Keep in mind that a seller is neither obliged nor probably willing to answer all this for you, so you might have to gain their confidence and slowly bring them to tell you what you might need to know.

Besides being informed about the seller and the state that the property is in, you also have to find out about the local market. How much are similar properties being sold for?

Discuss with the neighbors of properties that were sold recently. They might inform you on whether there were repairs made before the sale. While you're taking a look around, compare the condition of the property with that of others in the neighbourhood. An area may become sought after or avoided by people; this will have an effect on the property's price.

Having researched the market and the seller, ensure anything else that you need is ready before starting negotiations. Your financing should be ready, and cash in hand always appears safer than a promise.

It's advisable to make offers using figures that are not rounded up, for example $185,400. When the deal has to do with a lot of money, people tend to think in percentages. The difference is small between $185,400 and $185,000; however, $400 is still a significant sum. This practice also takes the other party by surprise, forcing them to wonder at your inscrutable pattern of thinking.

Your offer should be fair compared with the market average. An extremely low offer rejects you in the eyes of the seller, while an extremely high offer barely allows you any room to negotiate. Before starting, in any case, prepare your plan of action. Everything and anything can be part of the bargain. The price of property is only one of the many elements on the table.

You can bargain for the percentage of closing costs, for insurance, for the costs of the title, for realtor fees, for maintenance costs, etc. But, of course, don't expect to get everything you ask for.

When to Buy and When to Sell

Timing is essential in real estate investment, as in any other business. But there are two significant points which are different.

Other transactions in other businesses can be made in the space of minutes. The buying or the sale of real estate property happens in the space of months. This makes timing in buying and selling property quite crucial.

Just as elsewhere, the most profitable route is to sell high and plan to buy low later on. The time difference though, here, required to fulfill a transaction always alters the data on the table.

A stock can easily be sold, and after a week (or several) be bought back at a lower price. While its price keeps rising, there are others whose price will drop but is bound to rise again. Such occurrences are quite rare in the world of real estate.

The second point that sets apart real estate from other businesses is that in the latter, most companies are different and yet their stocks are alike. Real estate property is never similar to anything else, it is unique.

To sell in real estate you need first to buy a property and wait until the opportunity to sell appears, and then to buy again at a high price, in the hope of even greater profits. Meanwhile the costs of buying and selling are significantly larger than the minor costs of trading stock.

A positive outlook is always there because, historically, many have made great profits in real estate, and still do, despite the market going through circles in the last decades. This tells you that you should be thinking ahead, to the future.

You can do several things to better your timing. First, buy property at cheap prices, either by searching for foreclosures or taking up properties in need of significant repairs.

If you dedicate enough effort, you will discover foreclosures, which are sold in the range of between 25-35% under the current local market. Scan the local newspapers or sites for listings of "Notice of Default" and perhaps for auctions that might be taking place.

You may even discover places that sellers leave behind, but where the possibility exists for people to return. For example, specific neighborhoods in Manhattan having a bad reputation currently sell properties at maximum prices. Once more you will have to plan ahead and keep the future in mind.

If you're good with your hands or have the assistance of someone who would work for you without pay, you can obtain properties in need of repair. The price of a property may rise by ten percent, or even more, by having the leaks in the roof fixed, or by repairing damage caused by water.

An invaluable asset that will assist you with these is to have as much cash available as is possible. Of course, this doesn't translate into opening a big savings account. You will need to keep liquid, make sure your credit score is high, and build a healthy and trusting relationship with your lender to accommodate your financing.

The opportunity for profit arises even now when our market is quite still due to extremely high rates. But opportunity is for those who are patient, who can conduct a vast amount of research and are capable of dropping a deal when their expectations meet the disappointing facts.

What to Do When You Can't Sell

In the past it was easier to sell a property when price increases reached double-digit numbers. You sold the property at its market value or a bit higher and potential purchasers ran towards it, even in the space of a few days.

Every market has its ups and downs, real estate not being an exception. When prices start to stagnate, you may find your property in need of a potential purchaser who doesn't come calling. This is frustrating, keeps your capital tied up and doesn't permit you to make a profit. Don't act on impulse after being cornered. Reflect on what's the best move to make.

Even in such circumstances, a seller has a few moves available. If the property is also your home and you don't need to move out, you can just lie and wait for growth in the market. This might prove to be one or five years, but growth will definitely come.

If you're in waiting for a couple of months or a couple of years, still there exist trustworthy approaches you could take to increase your chances of attracting satisfactory bids.

Almost every property can use some improvements, and these are often cheap if you employ yourself for the task. Take up maintenance and restore the property to a better condition, even if the additional work doesn't serve a functional purpose but only an aesthetic one, by replacing carpets, repainting, repairing the lawn, cleaning and presenting your property in prime condition to potential buyers.

After you have the property looking and functioning as close to perfect as possible within the means of a small budget, engage people in your neighborhood to follow your example. The appearance of the area definitely reflects on your property.

When you have done everything possible to bring the property and its environment to optimal conditions, reflect on whether the price you have set is sensible. Prices change rapidly but also differ in various degrees even within a specific region. A story property of 2,500 square feet is of course going to be sold for less than a double-storey property of 3,000 square feet.

A price depends on the total square footage of the property, how old it is, etc. Compare properties on the internet to obtain a general idea, and then ask advice from a professional to obtain an estimate of the actual range within which the price of your property falls.

Solve problems such as noise from the street by installing double-glass windows, so that potential purchasers won't consider it a problem when they visit.

If your property has been on the market for a while but hasn't sold, it's advisable to remove it for some time, and then reflect again on its price when entering it in again. The majority of purchasers are suspicious towards something that hasn't been sold, even in the case when there is absolutely nothing wrong with it.

How much have you advertised? Make sure you have advertised within the local region where the property is but also online or in other places where you have a potentially attractive property. Employ modern technology in your favor and after this additional effort you will be rewarded.

Learning How to Flip

What is commonly called 'flipping' is buying a property and selling it rapidly in hopes of making a significant profit. It's legal and there are no ethical concerns, as it is part of the business.

Often confusion occurs between the practice of flipping and fraud exaggerating the value of a property through forging of documents and collaborating with other parties to present the purchaser with a fraud. The latter is unethical without question and illegal, but shouldn't be confused with flipping at all.

For you to flip a property, you usually need to have a "fixer-upper" and quickly conduct repairs on it, or find a seller who is keen to sell at a bargain price.

Investigate among friends and acquaintances, relatives and fellow workers, bankers, professionals in the real estate business, or any person who you think might lead you to a bargain. You might even be lucky enough to spot one while driving around in your car, paying attention to the signs "For Sale by Owner."

You might choose to conduct extensive research to discover owners unable to pay their mortgage. If you do and they sell to you, both parties are satisfied. You end up with a property that will generate profit for you, while they are rid of the burden of a debt they're unable to pay. So far, everything is legal and ethical about it.

In some agreements you're not even required to have your name on the title. You can do what is called "double escrowing," to a purchaser who wishes to continue living at his property. To do so you have to take an escrow for more than 90 days and sell the property during this time so that both agreements close escrow at the same time. In a market where prices increase swiftly, the purchaser may then make the most of the increase in the property's sale value.

You can also flip by agreeing to purchase a property and selling the contract to a different purchaser before the end of the escrow period. Your profit will range between $500 and $5,000, relieving you of the effort to attract financing.

To succeed in flipping, however, you have to learn the necessary skills and reflect on your type of personality.

You must understand how to discover a property that has the potential to be sold and to understand a purchaser's psychology. You should update yourself on property maintenance, and probably get involved in doing part of it yourself. That translates into learning about carpentry, plumbing, or other skills that you might not already have at the outset.

Furthermore, your character must be that of an active individual; flipping requires you to handle a great number of details in a very short time frame. It also demands a great tolerance against the pressure of risk. Purchasers under stress most often are not sensible or calm enough to sign an agreement with. They tend to have a mediocre credit score and are prone to give up on an agreement at the last moment.

You should improve your bargaining skills and build strong relationships with lenders, specifically those whom you can trust to assist you fast when you're in need of them. A reliable accountant is also worth having, as well as a cooperative attorney, unless of course you feel able to fulfil these roles yourself.

Foreclosure: a Lamb or a Wolf in Sheep's Clothing?

Ignorance is loss, and in our case financial loss. Predicting the future is your strongest skill when deciding if you should rent a property or whether it's better to sell it today for a standard profit.

If you wish to maintain possession of a property, plan to make the best of tax breaks and capital evaluation, but hope to outweigh the necessary expenses, reflect on both those positive points and on some probable negative points of renting.

Since the property belongs to you, by law you're responsible for all the standard costs revolving around the owner, whether they are payments of mortgages, insurance, taxes, or others. Furthermore, in almost all cases your contract will oblige you to pay for the necessary repairs or conduct them; that is, those repairs that are not a result of damage caused by a tenant. By common logic, not performing basic repairs on the property will create a feeling of hostility in the tenants against you, breaching the trust between you and inviting them to invent sideways approaches to avenge you. Hostile tenants also happen to have rights on their side.

Before things reach that point, plan ahead.

Compare the prospects of paying tax while keeping the property and selling. Plan an estimate, according to studies on the market and interest rates, to predict whether prices are about to rise or drop. If you decide to rent the property, do your research and be informed about your legal rights and your obligations.

Any tenant looking forward to residing within the property should complete an application, providing you with information and permitting you to conduct a fair amount of background checking. Look into their credit history, verify their employment status and call their previous landlords to discuss their behavior during tenancy.

Make sure the contract you prepare identifies your and the tenant's rights and responsibilities as clear as possible. Do not use obscure language, so no one may claim they fail to understand what is stated in the contract. Also, ensure that the contract is fair towards both you and the tenant. Note the necessary deposit that's required, how much notice you have to give before inspections, whether it is you or the tenant who is responsible for specific maintenance, etc.

Make sure you keep your part of the agreement, but also feel free to act even better. When a tenant requires you to act on repairs, make sure to do so in as little time as possible. You should never provide the tenants with a reason that would become their excuse for failure to pay the rent. Both you and they will benefit from mature behavior and treating each other with the necessary respect.

Be prepared to have enough insurance for major repairs that might arise; alternatively be ready to carry out the repairs yourself.

Your records of payment dates and financial sums should be accurate and up-to-date. Don't hesitate to discover why a tenant is late in paying the rent. It is only human to delay paying the rent for a couple of days, so do not worry. However, if a tenant is consistently late, you might need to start worrying.

Your approach should be to call the tenant and discuss the matter in a calm and professional manner. Remind the tenant that the contract allows you to assess a fee on late payments, so that this works towards encouraging them to be on time. Ensure you have good knowledge of the law before you happen to need it.

You could also check with the neighbors every now and then, in a warm and friendly manner, to find out whether the new tenant's behavior is fine. A tenant doesn't have to become friends with the rest of the neighborhood; however, if they are constantly creating problems for their neighbors, such as littering, damaging the property, making too much noise, and so forth, your property's value might be affected. Neighbors can inform you about inappropriate behavior of future tenants who have expressed an interest in renting your property.

In the case where you need to take legal action, your first step should be to opt for arbitration. This way problems tend to get resolved faster, cheaper, and most of the time all parties are happy with the result.

Renting a Property: a Dream or a Nightmare?

Ignorance is loss, and in our case financial loss. Predicting the future is your strongest skill when deciding if you should rent a property or whether it's better to sell it today for a standard profit.

If you wish to maintain possession a property, planning to make the best of taxation breaks and capital evaluation, but hope to outweigh the necessary expenses, reflect on both those positive points and on some probable negative points to renting.

Since the property belongs to you, by law you're responsible for all the standard costs revolving around the owner, whether they are payments of mortgages, insurance, taxes, or other. Furthermore, in almost all cases your contract will oblige you to pay for the necessary repairs or conduct them, that is, those repairs that are not a result of damage caused by a tenant. By common logic, not performing basic repairs in the property will create a feeling of hostility in the tenants against you, breaching the trust between you and inviting them to invent sideways approaches to avenge you. Hostile tenants, who also happen to have right on their side, are against you.

Before things though reach that point, plan ahead.

Compare the prospects of paying tax while keeping the property and selling. Plan an estimate, according to studies on the market and interest rates, to predict whether prices are about to rise or drop. If you decide to rent the property, make your research and be informed about your legal rights and your obligations.

Any tenant looking forward to residing within the property, should complete an application, providing you with information and permitting you to conduct a fair amount of background check. Look into their credit history, verify their employment status and call their previous landlords to discuss their behaviour during tenancy.

Make sure the contract you prepare identifies yours and the tenant's rights and responsibilities as clear as possible. Do not use obscure language, so no one may claim they fail to understand what is stated by the contract. Also, ensure that the contract is fair towards both you and the tenant. Note the necessary deposit required how much time notice you have to give before inspections, whether it is you or the tenant that is responsible for specific parts of maintenance, etc.

Make sure you keep your part of the agreement, but also feel free to act even better. When a tenant requires you to act for repairs, make sure to do so in as little time as possible. You should never provide the tenants with a reason that would become their excuse for failure to pay the rent. Both you and they will benefit from a mature behaviour and treating each other with the necessary respect.

Be prepared to have enough insurance for major repairs that might arise, alternatively be ready to carry out the repairs by yourself.

Your records of payment dates and financial sums should be accurate and up-to-date. Don't hesitate to discover why a tenant is late in paying the rent. It is only human to delay paying the rent for a couple of days, so do not worry. However, if a tenant is consistently late, you might need to start worrying.

Your approach should be to call the tenant and discuss the matter in a calm and professional manner. Remind the tenant that the contract allows you to fine a fee on late payments, so that this works towards encouraging them to be on time. Ensure you have good knowledge of the law before you happen to need it.

You could also check with the neighbours every now and then, in a friendly and approaching manner, to find out whether the new tenant's behaviour is fine. A tenant doesn't have to become friends with the rest, however, if they are constantly creating problems for their neighbours, such as littering, damaging the property, making too much noise, and so forth, your property's value might be affected. Neighbours can inform you on inappropriate behaviour of future tenants that have expressed an interest in renting your property.

In the case where you need to take legal action, you first step should be to opt for arbitration. This way problems tend to get solved faster, cheaper, and most of the time all parties are happy with the result.

The Complications of Commercial Investment

The Economist conducted a study recently, and found the investing in home property in developed countries amounted to the sum of forty eight trillion dollars. Meanwhile, investment in commercial real estate was fourteen trillion dollars. The latter number might seem low, yet investment in commercial real estate is a much more complicated business.

Unlike stocks or other businesses, real estate is always concentrated on location, since property always exists somewhere physically. The investor might be on the other side of the world, yet the property exists in a specific place which constitutes part of the general surrounding market.

Location, then, affects how a property is evaluated, bought, employed and sold. In contrast with home property, commercial property usually serves a business purpose.

Commercial investors often have to invest larger amounts of capital, and superior credit is required of them. They run a greater risk, and usually also have to evaluate capitalization rate and Gross Rent Multiplier.

To calculate the capitalization rate, one divides a property's annual income by its purchase value. Throughout history, investments have benefitted from a ten percent rate; however, in the last several years this has been reduced to eight per cent, as there are bigger risks involved and lower expectations on profits. The Gross Rent Multiplier can be calculated if one divides the purchase price by the property's monthly income. These numbers, together with the estimated value of a property, total income, etc. constitute the solid basis for determining the worth of an agreement.

Commercial properties run bigger risks of unforeseen change under standard financial circumstances. A construction which had a one hundred percent occupancy rate may find its percentage drop to half due to factors unrelated to the local market. Events that take place on the other side of the planet have the potential to alter business circumstances overnight, whether the tenants are located in London or Madrid.

Commercial property investment demands vast legal knowledge, as well as knowledge of repairs and finance. Because these properties are often rented instead of just bought and sold, their owners find themselves obliged to install extensive electric, air conditioning and security monitoring systems, apart from fire alarms, landlines and internet facilities. Even the outlay of plumbing becomes more complex within commercial constructions. Mortgages, as one would expect, present a far greater degree of complication, while insurance also is more expensive.

The triple-net lease is the only exception, since in this agreement the tenant is held responsible for all expenses and the costs of maintenance and repair, including as well the costs of insurance.

On the other hand, there's great profit to be made from commercial real estate investment. The risk might be higher; however, usually the profits are higher too, especially so while a good financial atmosphere lasts. In the end, sometimes, something that is more complicated is also all the more intriguing.

Taxation for Investors

Tax regulations are perhaps the most complex invention of man. In this regard, the following shouldn't be taken as legal advice. You should seek out the advice of your attorney or tax accountant before acting.

The first question on this subject is: What considerations should I, as a real estate investor, set out to make? Due to the difference in laws between different countries, any advice of a general nature would be useless. There are, however, a few specific details that are true for many areas.

A great number of investors think they could buy a home property, not live in it, make the necessary repairs and sell it making a significant profit. This is often the case. However, profits can be reduced if one is ignorant of the current laws on taxation. The regulation many forget applied solely to property that was used as a home residence in the U.S.A. is not still in effect.

This regulation was replaced in 1997 by another, which permitted the sale of a home property free of taxes, if it was occupied for two or more years. Income from investment, regardless of whether it's from stock sales or from real estate, is regarded as capital gain. If the property was kept for a year or less, it's then considered as short-term gain, which is taxed at ordinary rates, normally as high as 35%. If the property is kept longer than a year, any sale now is then regarded as a long-term, capital gain, which is taxed normally at about 15%. What this means is that one day in or out of the year could make a difference of 20% of value.

If one maintains the property for the number of 730 days as their home, then they don't have to pay tax at all, if the money is invested again in a home of equal or higher value.

If the investor isn't planning to live in the property, the alternative option in the U.S.A. is the 1031 exchange.

If you swap an investment or the property of a business for another of the same kind, you are allowed to defer any tax that you owe. The "same kind" is defined in rather loose terms. You may trade developed land for undeveloped land, a commercial property for a primary residence, and so forth. The only limit imposed is that the traded property must be an asset available to generate income.

Remember that this option isn't a way to avoid taxation but only to defer it and cannot be employed in conjunction with your primary residence. Seek out the advice of your tax accountant or attorney before determining to make the best of this regulation.

Married couples are entitled by tax law changes to profits reaching up to five hundred thousand dollars upon selling their primary residence, while singles are allowed two hundred and fifty thousand without a tax penalty.

Make sure to always maintain accurate records and to seek the advice of professionals before deciding to proceed in any investment. This goes for those fortunate enough to have obtained property by inheritance, or others who are involved in estate sales and trusts. It will be more worth paying their fees instead of penalties later on and unexpected taxes.

Real Estate or Paper Estate?

Evaluations and inspections, renters, advertising...all these sure manage to become a headache. Still though, real estate investment maintains its attractiveness and charm. What should you do? Think about the possibility of investing in real estate-based economic instruments.

Real Estate Investment Trusts: REITs are mutual funds which invest in real estate, in actual, "real" property, and in addition in mortgage portfolios. REITs conduct sales on the great exchanges, are managed by professionals, fall under special tax considerations, and most of the times have greater yields and higher liquidity than "common" property investment.

There exist Equity REITs, which invest in properties as well as own them. Their profits originate mostly from the rents they collect. Mortgage REITs invest and own mortgages instead of property, and their income is sourced primarily from interest on the loans. Hybrid REITs, the third category, are a mixture of both.

Don't forget, however, that REITs are mutual funds which have a specific number of shares for sale, and that once these shares are sold they cannot be redeemed through the REIT. One would have to buy and sell to other investors, in the same manner one would do with stock, through an individual broker or a firm.

REITs have to pay at least 90% of their profits to shareholders as dividends, so one can understand why they may be high yield. REITs are sensitive to changes in the interest rates; as interest rates go up, REIT prices show a tendency to drop.

Mortgage-Backed Securities: MBS is a kind of bond in which the paperwork is backed by a sum of mortgage loans. In the U.S.A. lenders make profits of about three trillion dollars in such loans every year, with almost 80% being covered by MBS.

If you're investing in mortgage securities, you earn a coupon rate of interest. But in contrast to when this happens with other types of bonds, here you receive repayments of the principle during the life of the security, while the mortgage loans are being paid off, instead of one large payment being made at maturity.

On the side of the positives, the statistical effect of a sum of loans offers the security a certain measure of stability. A small number of loans, or one single loan, cannot pre-pay default, nor can they wipe out the investor's entire investment.

However, pre-payment of mortgages takes place for a specific percentage and that in itself brings in a certain amount of risk. The investor doesn't know which loans pre-pay, or is not interested to find out; nevertheless the fact remains that some pre-pay causes them to become sensitive to changes in the interest rate. If borrowers received mortgages at 8%, for example, and rates dropped to 5%, then a specific number are going to be re-financed, causing the original to pay off before its time.

In conclusion, the best route is to steer away from pre-payable MBS if interest rates tend to drop. Closed MBS are perhaps a more advisable alternative scenario in the present case.

There exist also specialized instruments such as Collateralized Mortgage Obligations, and the Real Estate Mortgage Investment Conduits, which show a similar behavior and present similar potential risks. Fixed Income Exchange-Traded Funds, also, are sometimes supported by MBS and trade on the bigger stock markets. They are designed to check on the performance of certain indexes of bonds, which track in their turn the performance of underlying bond markets such as MBS.

Self-Directed Individual Retirement Accounts: You may set up an IRA, since it permits you to include assets in it such as raw land, family residences, apartments or buildings of commercial use, instead of cash, to make the most of your experience in real estate and at the same time avoid the negative sides of managing an actual property.

Any of these paths that you may choose, or others that exist, shouldn't stop you from doing your research and receiving advice from professionals before investing a large amount of money. There are always other parties ready to take advantage of you and your mistakes without a second thought.

We Want Your Feedback on This Book!

Our main purpose is to make sure that our readers get value from the books we publish and that they have a good experience with all of our products. We are always working to improve our books and other products with every revision and update.

Every piece of feedback makes a difference in this process. And we would appreciate yours as well - whether it is good or bad.

Please take one minute to let us know what you thought by following this link:

http://checkmateng.com/feedbackrealestateinvestng/

www.ingramcontent.com/pod-product-compliance
Lightning Source LLC
Chambersburg PA
CBHW071809170526
45167CB00003B/1239